THE BEST LITTLE
BBQ SAUCES
COOKBOOK

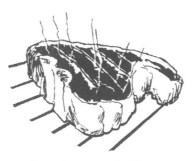

by Karen Adler

CELESTIALARTS
Berkeley, California

Special thanks to
Ardie Davis, Dave DeWitt, Mary Ann Duckers,
Don McLemore, Lou Jane Temple, Helen Willinsky
for their contributions to this book.

CELESTIALARTS
P.O. Box 7123
Berkeley, CA 94707

Printed in Singapore.

Cover design: Catherine Jacobes
Cover art: Paul Keppel
Interior illustrations: Barry's Clip Art, Basting brush by Brad Greene
Text design: Greene Design

Library of Congress Catalog Card Number: 00-131237

Other cookbooks in this series:
Best Little Barbecue Cookbook
Best Little Grilling Cookbook
Best Little Marinades Cookbook

Celestial Arts titles are distributed in Canada by Ten Speed Canada, in the United Kingdom and Europe by Airlift Books, in South Africa by Real Books, in Australia by Simon & Schuster Australia, and in New Zealand by Southern Publishers Group.

Introduction

Growing up in Kansas City, I had my first taste of barbecue at the tender age of seven. My father would leave his business downtown and take a circuitous route home on Friday afternoons. The reason for this detour was to pick up barbecue at Benny's on Blue Ridge Cut-Off. On his arrival, my mother would spread the goods from the paper sack onto the kitchen table. We would each grab a sandwich wrapped in white butcher paper and begin the feast. The wagon wheel sandwiches came in combinations of smoked beef brisket, pork, and/or ham on seeded kaiser rolls with plenty of warm tangy red sauce that had soaked into the bread on the drive home. There would also be a slab of ribs topped with dill pickle slices served Kansas City–style over plain white sandwich bread. My favorite finale to this simple all-American meal was to take a piece of the meat-soaked white bread and smother it in more of the fragrant warm barbecue sauce. It is still my favorite way to taste and eat barbecue sauce!

About Barbecue Sauce

Traditional American barbecue hails from five distinct regions of the United States: Kansas City, Texas, Memphis, and the Carolinas. Kansas City sauce is synonymous with thick, sweet, and tangy tomato-based barbecue sauce. Texas sauce is less sweet with a little more chile heat. Memphis typifies the Southern vinegar-based sauces where the punch of flavor comes from the rub rather than the sauce.

Finally the Carolinas bring several styles of sauce to the table. From South Carolina come the mustard-based sauces found in the central and southeastern regions of the state, the ketchup-based BBQ sauces come from along the Georgia border, the vinegar-based sauces hail from the northeast, and the tomato-based sauces or Williamsburg style come from the northwest. Sauces from North Carolina evolved in both the eastern and western parts of the state. There is the classic trinity of vinegar, salt, and pepper. Eastern North Carolina variations include vinegar, water, salt, black pepper, red pepper, finely ground cayenne, and dried crushed red pepper. There is no sweetener in this sauce, but some barbecuers like to add some sweet to the mixture when it is served as a dipping sauce. Early colonists considered the tomato poisonous, thus no tomato in the sauce. Another variation is to season the chopped pork dry with salt, black pepper, and red pepper, then moisten it with plain vinegar. Western North Carolina or Piedmont-style barbecue elaborates on the vinegar-salt-pepper theme by adding a little ketchup, Worcestershire sauce, and brown sugar to cut the bite and create the darker Lexington-style sauce. The term "pig picking" grew out of the casual get-together where the whole pig is brought off the grill onto the serving table, and guests literally pick the meat from the pig.

California-style, or West Coast sauces, use fresh herbs and citrus fruits and include bourbon-laden sauces that use Jack Daniel's or Jim Beam, microbrew sauces, and wine-based sauces that use Zinfandel, Cabernet, Merlot, and other wines for flavoring.

Asian-style barbecue sauces have been enthusiastically embraced on the West Coast and feature the exotic flavors of China, Thailand, Vietnam, Japan, Mongolia, and Indonesia.

There are also specialty sauces designed specifically for certain kinds of wild game or the white barbecue sauce from Alabama that is usually used for poultry but is also good on fish. New Mexico and the Southwest have added a sophisticated repertoire of sauces that include all kinds of chiles from mild jalapeños and smokey chipotles to fiery habaneros and African bird peppers. However, the tomato- and ketchup-based types still outsell all others.

Most traditional barbecue sauces have in common a sweetener, usually white or brown sugar, honey, or molasses. (Maple syrup and corn syrup are modern-day variations.) Because sugars tend to burn easily, sauces should be used only during the final stages of cooking: for slow low-temperature cooking, the last 30 to 60 minutes; for hot fast grilling, the last 5 minutes. This is especially true with tomato-based sauces, which will blacken long before the meat is done.

BBQ Sauce Recipes

Basic Barbeque Sauce

Although there are scores of commercially made sauces available today, homemade barbecue sauce is always the best barbecue sauce.

3 tablespoons vegetable oil

1 onion, finely chopped

1 green bell pepper, finely chopped

1 cup ketchup

1 cup tomato sauce

1 cup water

1/2 cup cider vinegar

2 tablespoons lemon juice

2 tablespoons molasses

1 tablespoon Worcestershire sauce

1 teaspoon cayenne pepper

1 teaspoon dry mustard

1/2 teaspoon liquid smoke

 In a large saucepan, heat oil and sauté the onion and bell pepper for about 3 to 5 minutes over medium heat. Add the remaining ingredients and simmer over low heat for 1 hour. Store in an airtight jar in the refrigerator for up to 2 weeks.

Makes 3 cups

Quick Sweet & Spicy BBQ Sauce

This is almost a no-cook sauce! It's perfect for making on a weekday night because of its simplicity.

2 cups tomato sauce

1 cup cider vinegar

1 cup brown sugar

1 large white onion, minced

6 tablespoons Dijon mustard

1 tablespoon dried thyme

1 teaspoon cayenne pepper

1 teaspoon seasoned black pepper

1/2 teaspoon salt

 In a large saucepan, combine all of the ingredients. Bring to a boil, then lower heat and simmer for 15 minutes to blend flavors. Store in an airtight jar in the refrigerator for up to 2 weeks.

Makes about 4 cups

Kansas City-Style BBQ Sauce

Kansas City barbecue sauce is tomato-based with a sweet and tangy flavor.

2 tablespoons butter

1 large onion, finely chopped

2 cloves garlic, minced

2 cups ketchup

1 cup tomato juice

1 cup brown sugar

1/2 cup molasses

1/4 cup cider vinegar

2 tablespoons Worcestershire sauce

3 or 4 dashes hot sauce

1 teaspoon freshly ground black pepper

1/2 teaspoon salt

In a large saucepan, melt butter and sauté onion and garlic over medium heat until translucent. Add the remaining ingredients and simmer for 1 hour. Store in an airtight jar in the refrigerator for up to 2 weeks.

Makes about 6 cups

Carolina Mustard Sauce

This unique mustard-based sauce complements pork, poultry, and sausages.

1 cup yellow mustard

1 cup vinegar, cider or red wine

1/3 cup sugar

2 tablespoons butter

1 tablespoon Worcestershire sauce

1 teaspoon black pepper

1/2 teaspoon white pepper

1/2 teaspoon Tabasco sauce

1/2 teaspoon salt

Combine all of the ingredients in a large saucepan. Simmer for 30 minutes over medium-low heat. Store in an airtight jar in the refrigerator for up to 2 weeks.

Makes about 2 cups

North Carolina Dipping Sauce

This Lexington-style or Piedmont-style vinegar-based sauce is traditionally served with chopped dry pork. The pork can be seasoned with salt and pepper, then moistened with vinegar, or you can use this sauce as a one-step method.

2 cups cider vinegar

2/3 cup ketchup

1/2 cup brown sugar

1 tablespoon Tabasco sauce

1 tablespoon Worcestershire sauce

1 teaspoon dry mustard

1 teaspoon red pepper flakes

1 teaspoon freshly ground black pepper

1 teaspoon onion salt

Combine all of the ingredients in a large saucepan. Simmer for 30 minutes over medium-low heat. Store in an airtight jar in the refrigerator for up to 2 weeks.

Makes about 3 cups

New Mexico-Style BBQ Sauce

This peppery barbecue sauce is especially nice on pork and poultry. Enjoy it as a welcome change of pace from the traditional tomato-based sauces that dominate American barbecue.

1/4 cup unsalted butter

1 red onion, finely diced

2 cloves garlic, finely diced

2 tablespoons dark brown sugar

2 tablespoons ancho chile powder

2 tablespoons pasilla chile powder

1 tablespoon Worcestershire sauce

1 teaspoon cayenne pepper

1/4 teaspoon oregano

1/4 teaspoon cumin

1/2 cup red wine vinegar

1/2 cup water

Sea salt to taste

 Melt butter in a heavy skillet over medium heat. Add onion and garlic and sauté for about 10 minutes until translucent. Add the remaining ingredients and simmer for 10 minutes. Store in an airtight container in the refrigerator for 1 week or in the freezer for several months.

Makes about 1¹/4 cups

SMOKEY CHIPOTLE SAUCE

Dave DeWitt is the guru of the chile pepper world. This is an adaptation of one of his excellent recipes.

4 dried chipotle chiles

1 cup boiling water

2 tablespoons butter

1 onion, finely chopped

1 clove garlic, minced

1/2 cup sour mash bourbon

1 cup ketchup

1/4 cup brown sugar

1/4 cup balsamic vinegar

1/4 cup lemon juice

2 tablespoons Worcestershire sauce

1 tablespoon ancho chile powder

2 teaspoons dry mustard

 Rinse chiles. Pour boiling water over chiles and let them rehydrate and soften for 30 minutes, then drain.

In a large saucepan, melt butter and sauté onion and garlic over medium heat until soft. Then add bourbon, lower heat to a simmer, and reduce by half. Add chiles and the remaining ingredients, bring to a boil, then reduce heat and simmer for at least 1 hour. Purée sauce in a blender until smooth. Store in an airtight container in the refrigerator for 3 to 4 weeks or in the freezer for several months.

Makes about 3 cups

Texan Beef Brisket Serving Sauce

A delicious barbecue sauce for beef brisket and beef ribs, but good on pork and chicken, too. Serve it warmed.

2 tablespoons olive oil

1 large onion, chopped

3 cloves garlic, minced

2 cups tomato sauce

1 cup chili sauce

1/4 cup brown sugar

2 tablespoons apple cider vinegar

2 tablespoons Worcestershire sauce

2 teaspoons cayenne pepper

1 teaspoon dry mustard

1 teaspoon ground black pepper

 Heat oil in a large sauté pan. Add onion and garlic and cook over medium-high heat for about 7 to 10 minutes, until lightly browned. Stir in the remaining ingredients and bring to a boil. Reduce heat and simmer for 1 hour. Strain sauce and discard solids. Store in an airtight jar in the refrigerator for several weeks.

Makes about 4 cups

CROSS-CULTURAL CALIFORNIA BARBECUE SAUCE

This sauce uses fresh herbs and a hint of Asian ingredients to create a California-style barbecue sauce.

2 tablespoons extra virgin olive oil

1 large white onion, finely chopped

2 cloves garlic, minced

1 cup chili sauce

1/2 cup dark honey

1/4 cup balsamic vinegar

1/4 cup Worcestershire sauce

2 tablespoons soy sauce

2 teaspoons wasabi powder or paste

1 Knorr beef bouillon cube

1 teaspoon chopped fresh oregano

1 teaspoon chopped fresh thyme

Sea salt and freshly ground black pepper to taste

In a large skillet, heat olive oil and sauté onion and garlic until translucent. Stir in the remaining ingredients and simmer for 30 minutes. Store in an airtight jar in the refrigerator for up to 3 weeks.

Makes about 3 cups

Big Bob Gibson's Alabama White Sauce

This recipe is courtesy of Don McLemore. His grandfather, Big Bob, created the original recipe, which is a thin white sauce usually served with smoked chicken and also good with fish.

1 cup mayonnaise

1 cup cider vinegar

1 tablespoon lemon juice

1 1/2 tablespoons cracked black pepper

1/2 teaspoon salt

1/4 teaspoon ground red pepper

 Combine all of the ingredients in a large glass jar with a tight-fitting lid. Close the lid and shake to blend. Store in the refrigerator for several weeks.

Makes about 2 cups

REMUS'S KANSAS CITY CLASSIC SAUCE

From Remus Powers, Ph.B., a.k.a. Ardie Davis, originator of the Diddy-Wa-Diddy Sauce Contest, now the International American Royal Barbecue Sauce Contest.

1/2 teaspoon curry powder, Oriental preferred

1/2 teaspoon chili powder

1/2 teaspoon paprika

1/4 teaspoon allspice

1/4 teaspoon cinnamon

1/4 teaspoon mace

1/4 teaspoon pepper

1/4 cup white vinegar

1 cup ketchup

1/3 cup dark molasses

1/2 teaspoon hot sauce

Place all the dry ingredients in a bowl. Add vinegar and stir. Add the remaining ingredients and stir until mixture is thoroughly blended. This sauce may be served at room temperature or warmed.

Makes 2 cups

Jamaican Jerk BBQ Sauce

Author Helen Willinsky's cookbook Jerk-Barbecue from Jamaica *has a delicious jerk marinade recipe that I have adapted to create a pungent and spicy barbecue sauce.*

1 cup ketchup

3 tablespoons soy sauce

1 onion, chopped

2 scallions, chopped

1 clove garlic, minced

2 tablespoons dark brown sugar

2 tablespoons distilled vinegar

2 teaspoons dried thyme

1 teaspoon allspice

1 teaspoon cinnamon

1 teaspoon freshly ground black pepper

1 teaspoon hot sauce

1/2 teaspoon freshly ground nutmeg

2 tablespoons dark rum

 In a food processor, combine all of the ingredients except the rum and process. Transfer mixture to a large saucepan and bring to a boil, then simmer the sauce over low heat until thick, about 10 minutes. Stir in the rum during the last 2 minutes. Store in an airtight jar in the refrigerator for up to 3 weeks.

Makes about 2 cups

Herb Garden BBQ Sauce

Jazzed-up barbecue sauce spread on sliced artisan bread makes a plain hamburger into something quite special.

1 cup of your favorite spicy tomato
   barbecue sauce

4 green onions, finely chopped

1 clove garlic, minced

1 tablespoon chopped fresh parsley

1 teaspoon lime or lemon juice

 Combine all of the ingredients in a glass jar with a tight-fitting lid. Shake to blend. Store in the refrigerator for up to 1 week.

Makes 1 cup

Sweet 'n Spicy Sauce from Remus Powers, Ph. B.

There are dozens of variations for tangy, tomato-based barbecue sauces. This one is a favorite.

1 cup ketchup

1 cup chili sauce

1 cup beef bouillon

1/2 cup Worcestershire sauce

1/3 cup orange juice

1/3 cup brown sugar, packed

1 onion, chopped

2 cloves garlic, minced

1 teaspoon Tabasco sauce or to taste

1/2 teaspoon liquid smoke

Combine all of the ingredients in a large saucepan. Simmer uncovered over low heat for 45 minutes to reduce sauce. Serve hot or cold.

Makes 4 cups

New and Improved Store-Bought Sauce

Commercially made barbecue sauce is very good and usually inexpensive. Buy several bottles of your favorites and create a trio of variations for your next backyard barbecue.

2 cups of your favorite bottled barbecue sauce

1/2 cup dark brown sugar

1/3 cup minced onion

5 large cloves garlic, minced

 Mix together all of the ingredients. Use immediately.

Makes about 2 1/2 cups

VARIATIONS:

Asian-Style BBQ Sauce: add 2 tablespoons soy sauce, 1 teaspoon ground ginger, 1 teaspoon garlic powder

Raspberry BBQ Sauce: add 1 package of frozen red raspberries in syrup

Bourbon-Que Sauce: add $1/4$ cup bourbon

Mustard-Style BBQ Sauce: add 1 cup yellow mustard

Border BBQ Sauce

Throw a handful of soaked mesquite chips on your charcoal fire to add the final ingredient to this zesty Southwest-style sauce. It's great with shrimp, chicken, beef, and pork.

1/2 cup spicy tomato barbecue sauce

1/2 bunch fresh cilantro, chopped

2 teaspoons fresh lime juice

Combine all of the ingredients in a glass bowl and serve as a dipping sauce. Use immediately.

Makes about 1 cup

Shrimp BBQ Sauce

*Drizzle this sauce over a grilled shrimp salad.
Add a squeeze of lemon or lime juice for a
final taste sensation.*

¼ cup Italian salad dressing

¼ cup of your favorite barbecue sauce

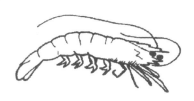 Combine the ingredients in a glass bowl
and use to marinate shrimp for 30 minutes.

Makes ½ cup

Que Sauce for Poultry

Adapted from The Passion of Barbeque, *the first barbecue cookbook published by Pig Out Publications, Inc., this is a delicious sauce to baste on grilled chicken and to serve on the side.*

1 red bell pepper, finely chopped

1 red onion, finely chopped

1 cup ketchup

1/2 cup water or more to thin sauce, as necessary

1/4 cup olive oil

1/4 cup chili sauce

1/4 cup lemon juice

2 tablespoons Worcestershire sauce

2 tablespoons steak sauce

2 tablespoons snipped fresh chives

2 tablespoons snipped fresh parsley

2 tablespoons honey

2 cloves garlic, minced

1 teaspoon chili powder

1 teaspoon paprika

1 teaspoon dry mustard

1 teaspoon seasoned black pepper

1 teaspoon salt

1/2 teaspoon cayenne pepper

 In a large saucepan, combine all of the ingredients and simmer for 1 1/2 hours over low heat. Store in an airtight jar in the refrigerator for up to 1 week.

Makes about 3 1/2 cups

Screaming Hot Sauce

Be warned—this sauce is really hot!

1 cup (2 sticks) butter

1 cup cider vinegar

1/3 cup prepared mustard

1 tablespoon red pepper flakes

1 tablespoon cayenne pepper

 In a small saucepan, melt butter over low heat. Stir in vinegar, mustard, and peppers. Let sauce cool, then pour sauce into a glass jar with a tight-fitting lid. Store in the refrigerator for up to several weeks.

Makes about 2 1/3 cups

Triple Red Pepper Sauce

This is a beautiful bright red salsa that packs a kick of heat.

1 can (10 ounces) diced Rotel tomatoes

1 red bell pepper, roasted and finely chopped

3 tablespoon lemon juice

1/2 tablespoon red pepper flakes

2 teaspoons cayenne pepper

1 teaspoon Tabasco or your favorite hot sauce

Place all of the ingredients in a large saucepan. Simmer for about 15 to 20 minutes over low heat. Serve as a hot and spicy side sauce for the meat of your choice. Store in an airtight jar in the refrigerator for up to 2 weeks.

Makes about 1 1/2 cups

CLASSIC COCKTAIL SAUCE

*Serve this with grilled shellfish, poultry,
or spicy meatballs.*

3/4 cup chili sauce

2 tablespoons white vinegar

1 tablespoon horseradish

1 tablespoon grated onion

1 teaspoon Worcestershire sauce

1/2 teaspoon Tabasco sauce

 Combine all of the ingredients in a glass
jar with a tight-fitting lid and stir to blend.
Store in the refrigerator for up to 2 weeks.

Makes about 1 cup

SPICY KETCHUP-MUSTARD SAUCE

This sauce is delicious and a snap to make.
Serve it with Asian-style grilled pork tenderloin
or smoked pork loin. It is also great with
French fries!

1 cup ketchup

2 tablespoons dry mustard

2 tablespoons cider vinegar

1 teaspoon curry powder

Combine all of the ingredients in a glass jar
with a tight-fitting lid. Store in the refrigerator
for up to 4 weeks.

Makes about 1 1/4 cups

Maple Bourbon Sauce

Use this sauce as a glaze or serve as a side sauce with wild game birds and venison.

1/2 cup bourbon

1 cup ketchup

1/2 cup maple syrup

1/4 cup vegetable oil

2 tablespoons cider vinegar

2 tablespoons Dijon mustard

In a large saucepan, reduce bourbon by half over medium-high heat. Remove from heat and add the remaining ingredients, stirring to blend. Store in an airtight jar in the refrigerator for up to 2 weeks.

Makes about 2 1/4 cups

Bourbon BBQ Sauce

Try this sauce on slow-smoked brisket and spareribs.

1 small onion, chopped
1 tablespoon olive oil
1 cup ketchup
1 cup chili sauce
$1/2$ cup orange marmalade
$1/4$ cup bourbon
$1/4$ cup cider vinegar
1 tablespoon Tabasco sauce
2 tablespoons Dijon mustard
2 teaspoons Worcestershire sauce
1 teaspoon ground pepper

Sauté onion in oil in a large saucepan over medium heat. Add the remaining ingredients and bring to a boil. Lower heat and simmer for about 30 minutes, stirring often until thickened.

Makes about 3 cups

CARPACCIO SAUCE

A delicious sauce to serve with very rare grilled meats and seafood like beef tenderloin and tuna steaks.

2 cups packed fresh parsley

$1/4$ cup capers

12 gherkins

3 anchovy fillets

2 cloves garlic, minced

3 tablespoons chopped onion

$1/4$ cup white wine vinegar

$1/3$ cup Dijon mustard

$3/4$ cup olive oil

2 tablespoons capers for garnish

 In a food processor, combine parsley, $1/4$ cup capers, gherkins, anchovies, garlic, onion, vinegar, and mustard. Slowly add olive oil in a thin stream to incorporate. Remove from processor and stir in the remaining 2 tablespoons capers. Serve immediately.

Makes $1^1/2$ cups

BÉARNAISE SAUCE

Béarnaise is traditionally served with meat, fish, eggs, or vegetables.

½ cup (1 stick) unsalted butter

2 tablespoons hot water

3 egg yolks

¼ cup tarragon vinegar

¼ cup dry white wine

1 tablespoon chopped fresh tarragon

½ tablespoon chopped fresh parsley

¼ teaspoon salt

¼ teaspoon Tabasco

In a double boiler, melt butter slowly over medium flame. Whisk in hot water and remove top of double boiler from the heat to cool. Place top of double boiler back on pot. Whisk in egg yolks and then the remaining ingredients. Over low heat, stir constantly until thick.

Makes about 1½ cups

Chimichurri Sauce-Marinade

This Argentinian steak sauce is traditionally served with pit-smoked beef. Besides being excellent for flavor, and completely natural, this marinade works wonders with tough beef. The results are amazing—enjoy!

1/2 cup olive oil

1/4 cup red wine vinegar

4 cloves garlic, chopped

2 teaspoons chopped fresh parsley

1 teaspoon dried oregano

1 teaspoon red pepper flakes

Salt and freshly ground black pepper to taste

 Combine all of the ingredients in a jar with lid. Let stand at room temperature for 1 day, or warm to about 120 degrees F for 1 to 2 minutes, then let stand for 1 hour to blend. Place meat and marinade in plastic bag for 1 hour before grilling. Store in an airtight jar in the refrigerator for up to 2 weeks.

Makes about 2/3 cup

Pacific Rim Vinegar Sauce

Baste grilled seafood or poultry with this sauce.
It is also a tasty finishing sauce to drizzle over a grilled
vegetable or meat salad.

1/4 cup dark rum

1 cup rice wine vinegar

1/2 cup freshly squeezed orange juice

1/2 cup dark brown sugar

Zest from 1 lime

2 tablespoons lime juice

2 tablespoons Thai chili sauce

1 tablespoon freshly grated ginger

2 teaspoons dry mustard

In a large saucepan, reduce rum by half over medium-high heat. Add the remaining ingredients and cook over medium-low heat for 20 to 30 minutes. Store in an airtight jar in the refrigerator for up to 2 weeks.

Makes about 2 cups

Harissa Sauce

This North African hot sauce is traditionally served with grilled lamb or kabobs.

2 sweet red bell peppers

4 or 5 fresh hot peppers

1 tablespoon butter

1 cup chopped Italian plum tomatoes,
    (fresh or canned)

3 tablespoons chopped fresh Italian parsley

1 tablespoon olive oil

1 tablespoon fresh lemon juice

1 teaspoon ground coriander

1 1/2 teaspoons ground cumin

Salt to taste

 Preheat oven to 375 degrees F. Roast the peppers by placing them in the oven for about 20 minutes or until they are charred and blistered. Place in a brown paper bag. Close the bag and allow peppers to steam for about 10 minutes to loosen skins. Remove from bag. Peel, remove seeds and stems, and finely mince peppers.

In a medium saucepan, melt butter. Add the peppers and sauté for 3 to 4 minutes. Add the remaining ingredients.

Store in an airtight jar in the refrigerator for up to 2 weeks.

Makes about 2¹/₂ cups

SPICY VINEGAR SAUCE

This is a traditional Carolina sauce to use as a condiment for pulled pork sandwiches, but it's also good on steamed spinach, German potato salad, hot bacon slaw, and wilted lettuce.

1 quart white vinegar

1/3 cup crushed red pepper flakes

1/3 cup sugar

1 1/2 tablespoons sea salt

 Combine all of the ingredients in a glass bowl and let stand at room temperature for several hours for flavors to blend. Pour into a plastic squirt bottle. Store indefinitely in the refrigerator.

Makes 1 quart

CHIVE-SHALLOT VINAIGRETTE

Serve this warm vinaigrette drizzled over a grilled shellfish or seafood salad. It is also a great basting mixture for meats and vegetables.

4 shallots, finely chopped

3 cloves garlic, minced

4 tablespoons butter

4 tablespoons white wine vinegar

1 tablespoon lemon juice

2 tablespoons snipped chives

1 tablespoon snipped Italian parsley

1/2 cup olive oil

Sauté shallots and garlic in butter over medium-low heat until soft for about 5 minutes. Add vinegar, lemon juice, chives, and parsley and sauté for 2 minutes more. Whisk in olive oil, then remove from heat. Store in an airtight jar in the refrigerator for up to 5 days.

Makes about 1 1/4 cups

ISLAND VINAIGRETTE

This is a tropical fruit baste or finishing sauce to pair with grilled poultry, pork, seafood, or fruits.

1/3 cup rice wine vinegar

2 tablespoons pineapple juice

2 tablespoons guava juice

2 tablespoons orange-flavored liqueur

1 tablespoon dark brown sugar

1 teaspoon almond extract

1 teaspoon minced fresh ginger

3/4 cup garlic oil

4 basil leaves, finely cut

Combine and blend vinegar, fruit juices, liqueur, brown sugar, almond extract, and ginger in a medium-size glass bowl. Slowly whisk in garlic oil to incorporate. Gently stir in basil. Use immediately.

Does not keep well.

Makes about 1 1/2 cups

Wildflower Honey Vinaigrette

Wildflower honey is a rich, dark golden honey gathered from bees that have feasted on wild prairie flowers. The lushness of this vinaigrette goes well with grilled lobster and other shellfish. It is a delightful dressing for mixed salad greens, too.

1/3 cup wildflower honey, warmed

1/3 cup raspberry vinegar

1 tablespoon seasoned pepper

1 teaspoon onion salt

2 cloves garlic, minced

1/4 cup finely minced mint

1 cup olive oil

Combine all of the ingredients in a wide-mouth glass jar, except the olive oil. Cover the jar and shake the ingredients to blend. Remove the lid and slowly whisk in the olive oil.

Store refrigerated for up to 1 week. Will keep longer if the fresh mint is added just before serving.

Makes about 2 cups

MEDITERRANEAN DIPPING SAUCE

Use this sauce as a bruschetta topping to serve alongside grilled vegetables and meats. Lightly grill French bread slices and rub each piece with a clove of garlic. Spread the Mediterranean Dipping Sauce on the grilled bread and place on a baking tray at 400 degrees F for several minutes, or until golden.

¼ cup mayonnaise

¼ cup freshly grated Parmesan cheese

2 tablespoons finely chopped green onion

2 tablespoons finely chopped black olives

1 clove garlic, minced

Pinch of ground red pepper

 Combine all of the ingredients in a small bowl and let the flavors blend for at least 30 minutes before using. Store in an airtight jar in the refrigerator for up to 5 days.

Makes about ³/4 cup

Basting Sauce for Poultry or Pork

This excellent vinaigrette-style basting sauce also makes a great marinade.

1/2 cup olive oil

1/3 cup vinegar

2 tablespoons Worcestershire sauce

2 tablespoons lemon juice

2 tablespoons honey

2 cloves garlic, minced

1 teaspoon freshly grated ginger

1 teaspoon ground coriander

1 teaspoon ground cumin

Place all of the ingredients in a large glass jar with a tight-fitting lid. Shake to blend. Store in the refrigerator for up to 1 month.

Makes about 1 1/3 cups

ROASTED RED PEPPER PESTO

The flavors of this pesto are a little sweeter than a regular basil pesto. It is wonderful on pork, chicken, seafood, bruschetta, and pizza.

1 cup roasted red peppers

1 cup packed fresh basil leaves

1/2 cup pine nuts

8 cloves garlic, minced

1 teaspoon black pepper

1/2 teaspoon sea salt

1/4 cup olive oil

1/4 cup Romano cheese

 In a food processor, combine red peppers, basil, pine nuts, garlic, pepper, and salt. Process by pulsating for about 20 to 30 seconds to finely chop ingredients. Then add oil and process for another 15 seconds to form a paste. Transfer to a bowl and stir in the cheese. Chill until ready to serve.

Does not keep well.

Makes about 2 cups

BBQ SAUCES

GREEK ISLE RELISH

Serve alongside your favorite grilled meat. This is especially complementary with lamb.

1 large ripe tomato, finely chopped

4 ounces feta cheese, crumbled

2 tablespoons finely chopped red onion

2 tablespoons chopped black olives

1 teaspoon red wine vinegar

1 teaspoon olive oil

1/2 teaspoon dried oregano

Combine all of the ingredients in a glass bowl and stir to blend. Let marinate for at least 30 minutes before using. Store in the refrigerator for up to 3 days.

Makes about 1 1/2 cups

Fiesta Relish

Fresh garden relishes are versatile. They can be served as salads, as sides to accompany meats, or as bruschetta or crostini toppings.

¼ cup chopped tomato

¼ cup chopped fresh cilantro

¼ cup chopped jalapeño pepper

¼ cup chopped green onion

Combine all of the ingredients in a small bowl and let flavors blend at least 30 minutes before using. Store in the refrigerator for up to 2 days.

Makes 1 cup

Thai Peanut Dipping Sauce

Serve this sauce with grilled pork tenderloin, lamb, or chicken. Or spread it on crusty French bread and make a Thai-style club sandwich with grilled chicken breast, golden fried bacon, and crisp green lettuce.

1/4 cup crunchy peanut butter

1/4 cup rice wine vinegar

1/4 cup soy sauce

2 tablespoons brown sugar

1 teaspoon sesame oil

1/2 teaspoon ground ginger

Combine all of the ingredients in a glass bowl and whisk to blend. Store in an airtight jar in the refrigerator for up to 3 weeks.

Makes about 3/4 cup

Thai Serving Sauce

This is an excellent serving sauce with lamb, pork, and poultry.

1/2 cup Dijon mustard

1/2 cup peanut butter

1/2 cup coconut milk

1/2 cup chopped peanuts

1/2 cup chopped green onions

 Combine all of the ingredients and use as a serving sauce. Store in an airtight container in the refrigerator for up to 2 weeks.

Makes 2 1/2 cups

SIMPLE SATAY SAUCE

This is a fresh and fabulous sauce to use as a baste or to serve alongside grilled shrimp and scallops. It pairs well with poultry and pork, too.

2 tablespoons soy sauce

4 tablespoons fresh lime juice

4 cloves garlic, minced

Combine all of the ingredients in a small glass bowl. You can make this recipe in larger quantities and store in the refrigerator for up to 1 week.

Makes about 1/3 cup

Sesame Soy Sauce

Soy sauce is a versatile base to marinades and serving sauces. This recipe is delicious with chicken and pork satay.

2/3 cup rice vinegar

1/3 cup soy sauce

2 cloves garlic, minced

1 teaspoon sesame oil

1/2 teaspoon five-spice powder

 Combine all of the ingredients in a glass bowl and serve as a dipping sauce.

Makes 1 cup

SZECHUAN SAUCE

This is a delicious hot dipping sauce for shrimp, scallops, and prawns. For extra heat, marinate and baste with a portion of the sauce.

1 cup bottled Szechuan sauce

¼ cup rice vinegar

¼ cup soy sauce

¼ cup dry vermouth

¼ cup honey, warmed

1 tablespoon minced ginger

Combine all of the ingredients in a glass jar with a tight-fitting lid and shake to blend. Store in the refrigerator for up to several weeks.

Makes 2 cups

AIOLI

*This is a garlic-flavored homemade mayonnaise
from Provence. It is traditionally served with a
platter of assorted steamed vegetables. Americanize
it by serving it with a platter of grilled vegetables
and meats.*

4 fresh organic egg yolks

4 to 6 cloves garlic, minced

1/4 teaspoon sea salt

1/4 teaspoon freshly ground black pepper

1 1/2 cups extra-virgin olive oil

 In a food processor, combine egg yolks, garlic,
salt, and pepper. Slowly add olive oil to incorporate.
Store in the refrigerator for up to 3 days.

Makes about 1 3/4 cups

QUICK ASIAN-STYLE BARBECUE SAUCE

Quick and simple recipes with no more than four ingredients are a lifesaver for busy people. When you have extra time, add minced fresh ginger, toasted sesame seeds, and snipped lemongrass to this recipe for added zest.

1 cup of your favorite tomato-based barbecue sauce

2 tablespoons soy sauce

1 teaspoon sesame oil

1 teaspoon ground ginger

Combine all of the ingredients and refrigerate. Serve hot or cold, on the side, or as a baste during the last 10 to 15 minutes of grill time.

Makes about 1 cup

ROUILLE

Rouille is a tomato-and-red-pepper-flavored French mayonnaise that is traditionally served with fish soup. It is excellent served alongside grilled seafood, pork, and poultry.

4 fresh organic egg yolks

4 to 6 cloves garlic, minced

1 fresh serrano chile pepper, cored, seeded, and minced

2 teaspoons sun-dried tomato paste

1/2 teaspoon sea salt

1/4 teaspoon freshly ground black pepper

1 cup olive oil

 In a food processor, combine egg yolks, garlic, chile pepper, tomato paste, salt, and pepper. Slowly add olive oil to incorporate. Store in the refrigerator for up to 3 days.

Makes about 1 1/4 cups

CAVIAR MAYONNAISE

For a festive occasion, serve this decadent sauce with a platter of grilled or steamed vegetables.

1/2 cup mayonnaise

2 tablespoons lemon juice

2 tablespoons salmon caviar

Combine mayonnaise and lemon juice, then gently stir in caviar. Refrigerate to chill. Serve with grilled lobster tails.

Makes about 3/4 cup

Spicy Horseradish Sauce

The pungent flavors of this concoction complement plain meats and fish like chicken, game hens, catfish, and shellfish.

1 cup light sour cream

4 tablespoons horseradish

2 tablespoons chopped pimiento

1 tablespoon paprika

1 teaspoon ground cumin

1 teaspoon allspice

1/2 teaspoon coriander

1/2 teaspoon red pepper flakes

 Combine all of the ingredients in a glass bowl. Refrigerate for 1 hour before serving. Store in the refrigerator for up to 3 days.

Makes about 1 1/2 cups

Extra Quick Horseradish Sauce

Serve this creamy, mild sauce with grilled or smoked beef.

2 cups whipped cream

2 tablespoons horseradish

 Blend together whipped cream and horseradish. Refrigerate until ready to serve.

Makes about 2 cups

Whiskey Cream Sauce

*Serve this whiskey sauce with smoked salmon,
poultry, beef, or wild game.*

1 bunch green onions
4 tablespoons butter
1/2 cup whiskey
1 cup whipping cream
2 tablespoons horseradish
2 tablespoons fresh minced Italian parsley
1/2 teaspoon sea salt
1/2 teaspoon freshly ground black pepper

 Snip the green part of the onions and set
aside. Finely mince the white part of the onions
and sauté in butter in a medium-size skillet until
soft. Add whiskey and cook over medium heat
until reduced by half. Add cream and horseradish
and heat until the mixture coats a spoon. Add
parsley, salt, pepper, and the green part of the
onions. Serve immediately.

Does not keep well.

Makes about 1 1/4 cups

Confetti Pepper Cheese

*Serve a dollop of this colorful cream cheese mixture
on top of grilled steak or chicken. It's a tasty base spread
for grilled pizza, too.*

8 ounces light cream cheese, room temperature

2 cloves garlic, minced

2 tablespoons finely chopped red bell pepper

2 tablespoons finely chopped yellow bell pepper

2 tablespoons chopped fresh parsley

2 tablespoons chopped fresh chives

2 tablespoons butter, softened

2 tablespoons lemon juice

1 tablespoon finely chopped jalapeño pepper

1 teaspoon coarsely ground black pepper

1/2 teaspoon white pepper

Pinch of salt

Combine all of the ingredients in a small bowl and blend
with a fork or mixer. Let flavors blend at least 30 minutes
before using. Store in the refrigerator for up to 1 week.

Makes about 1 3/4 cups

HERBED CREAM CHEESE

When basil, parsley, and chives are at their peak and plentiful, make this Provençal-style cheese spread.

1 package (8 ounces) light cream cheese, softened
1 can (4 ounces) chopped black olives
2 tablespoons chopped fresh basil
1 tablespoon chopped fresh parsley
1 tablespoon snipped fresh chives
1 clove garlic, minced

Combine all of the ingredients and blend. Serve with grilled hamburgers, sausages, or chicken as a spread for sandwiches.

Makes 1 cup

BLUE CHEESE SAUCE

This is delicious as a dipping sauce for poultry or grilled or raw vegetables.

4 ounces blue cheese, crumbled

1/2 cup light mayonnaise

1/2 cup light sour cream

1/2 teaspoon Tabasco sauce

1/4 teaspoon seasoned pepper

Combine all of the ingredients in a blender or food processor. Blend until smooth. Store in the refrigerator for up to 1 week.

Makes about 1 cup

HERB BUTTER

Herb butters are so easy to make, and they freeze well, too. Add onion or garlic for extra zestiness.

1 cup (2 sticks) unsalted butter

1 tablespoon finely chopped herbs
   (tarragon, parsley, basil, oregano, etc.)

Let butter come to room temperature. In a blender or food processor blend with herbs of your choice. Store in the refrigerator for about 1 week or in the freezer for about 1 month.

Makes 1 cup

ROQUEFORT APPLE-BACON BUTTER

Serve as a side condiment with beef or game.

1/2 cup (1 stick) butter softened

2 tablespoons crumbled Roquefort cheese

1 teaspoon Worcestershire sauce

2 slices apple-bacon, cooked crisp

1 tablespoon minced onion

1 tablespoon chopped chives

Combine butter, Roquefort, and Worcestershire sauce and cream until fluffy. Add bacon, onion, and chives and refrigerate to chill.

Makes about 3/4 cup

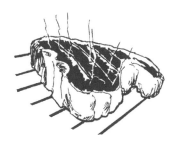

ROSEMARY BUTTER

Flavored butters are easy to make. For a myriad of variations, substitute the rosemary with the herb of your choice. Serve a pat of this butter atop grilled meats or vegetables.

1/2 cup (1 stick) butter, room temperature

2 teaspoons crushed rosemary

1 clove garlic, minced

Cracked pepper to taste

 Whip butter with rosemary, garlic, and pepper. Wrap butter in plastic wrap and shape into a log. Store in the freezer for several months. To serve, slightly thaw and slice.

Makes 1/2 cup

Three-Pepper Butter

Compound butters can be made ahead and stored in the freezer. They can be served with grilled meats and vegetables of your choice. They are also a nice base for bruschetta.

1/2 cup (1 stick) butter, softened

1 fresh red New Mexican chile, minced

1 tablespoon minced red onion

1/2 teaspoon paprika

1/4 teaspoon red pepper

1/4 teaspoon sea salt

In a small bowl, combine all of the ingredients and thoroughly blend. Place butter on a square of plastic wrap and shape into a log the size of a large coin. Place in a sealable freezer bag for storage. Slice pats of the butter when ready to serve. Store in the freezer for up to 3 months.

Makes about 1/2 cup

Gingersnap Sauce

This is delicious with beef and red game meat.

1 cup au jus or brown gravy

1/3 cup red wine

1/4 cup finely crushed gingersnaps

1/4 cup raisins (optional)

1/4 cup sliced almonds, toasted

1 teaspoon dark brown sugar

In a small saucepan, combine all of the ingredients. Simmer and stir over medium-low heat for about 7 minutes or until heated through. Serve immediately. Store in an airtight jar in the refrigerator for up to 1 week.

Makes about 2 cups

Sesame-Citrus Sauce

Serve this sauce with the seafood of your choice.
It is also excellent with grilled freshwater fish like
trout, bass, and catfish.

1/2 cup tahini (sesame paste)

1/2 cup plain yogurt

1 tablespoon lemon juice

1 tablespoon lime juice

1 tablespoon rice vinegar

2 cloves garlic, minced

1/2 teaspoon Tabasco sauce or to taste

1 lime, quartered for garnish

1 teaspoon toasted sesame seeds for garnish

Combine all of the ingredients, reserving the lime quarters and sesame seeds. Squeeze lime quarters over grilled fish. Spoon sauce over fish and sprinkle with a few sesame seeds for garnish. Store in the refrigerator for up to a few days.

Makes about 1 1/2 cups

Lemon-Herb Butter Baste

This is the perfect basting sauce for chicken and fish.

1/2 cup (1 stick) butter

2 tablespoons lemon juice

1 or 2 cloves garlic, minced

1/2 teaspoon fresh oregano

1/2 teaspoon fresh thyme

1/4 teaspoon fresh chopped rosemary

Salt and white pepper to taste

In a small saucepan, melt butter. Add the remaining ingredients and stir until blended.

Makes about 1 cup

Floribbean-Style Finishing Sauce

This unusual barbecue sauce includes horseradish and grapefruit juice (lime juice is a nice variation, too). It is tangy and sweet, with a delicate taste but a short shelf life. It's also an excellent basting sauce for fish and chicken.

¼ cup cider vinegar

¼ cup fresh grapefruit juice

¼ cup firmly packed dark brown sugar

1 can (6 ounces) tomato paste

2 tablespoons prepared horseradish

1 tablespoon capers

½ teaspoon cayenne pepper

½ cup olive oil

In a food processor, combine vinegar, grapefruit juice, brown sugar, tomato paste, horseradish, capers, and cayenne. Slowly add oil in a thin stream and continue to process until well blended. May be used as a marinade, basting sauce, or serving sauce. Store in an airtight container in the refrigerator for up to 3 days.

Makes 2 cups

Pepper Jelly Glaze

Baste poultry or pork with this glistening red sauce and reserve some to serve on the side.

1/2 cup currant jelly or pepper jelly

1/2 cup apple juice

2 teaspoons cornstarch

1/2 teaspoon celery salt

1/4 teaspoon dried red pepper flakes

In a small saucepan, combine all of the ingredients and cook over medium-high heat, stirring constantly until it boils. Store in an airtight jar in the refrigerator for up to 2 weeks.

Makes 1 cup

Southwestern Citrus Barbecue Sauce

Use this sauce as a finishing glaze or serving sauce for poultry, pork, or seafood. To extend the shelf life for up to 2 weeks, add the fresh cilantro as served.

1 tablespoon vegetable oil

1 large white onion, chopped

1 cup orange juice

1/2 cup lime juice

2 tablespoons brown sugar

1 tablespoon snipped fresh cilantro

1/2 teaspoon ground red pepper

1/2 teaspoon salt

Heat oil in a large sauté pan, add onion and sauté for about 5 minutes. Stir in the remaining ingredients. Bring to a boil, then reduce heat to low, and simmer uncovered for about 15 minutes, stirring occasionally. Store in the refrigerator for up to 3 days.

Makes about 2 cups

BLUEBERRY CITRUS SAUCE

An excellent accompaniment to grilled veal, game, and poultry.

1 cup blueberries, fresh or frozen

2 tablespoons sugar

2 tablespoons lemon juice

2 tablespoons vermouth

2 tablespoons grated orange peel

2 tablespoons grated lemon peel

1 tablespoon fresh minced ginger

 In a small saucepan, combine all of the ingredients. Bring to a boil over medium-high heat. Blueberries will begin to pop open and mixture will thicken. Remove from heat and serve warm, or refrigerate and serve cold. Store in the refrigerator for up to 1 week.

Makes about 1¹/₄ cups

Fruity BBQ Glaze

Blueberry, raspberry, cherry, and apricot preserves are a few of my favorites for this quick and easy glaze.

1 cup of your favorite barbecue sauce

1/4 cup fruit preserves

 Combine the ingredients in a small bowl. Use as a glaze for pork or poultry. Store in an airtight jar in the refrigerator for up to 2 months.

Makes 1 1/4 cups

Tangerine Glaze

1 can (6 ounces) tangerine juice

3 ounces frozen pineapple juice concentrate

2 tablespoons dark honey

2 tablespoons teriyaki sauce

1 teaspoon minced fresh ginger

 Combine all of the ingredients in a glass jar and blend well. Glaze meats during the last 10 minutes of grilling, or fish during the last 5 minutes of grilling. Store in the refrigerator for up to 2 weeks.

Makes about 1 1/4 cups

FRESH CRANBERRY-ORANGE RELISH

Fresh cranberries are available only in the winter. Make a double or triple batch of this recipe and store in 1-cup servings in individual freezer bags. Serve this relish with smoked meats.

2 navel oranges

2 1/2 cups fresh cranberries

3/4 cup sugar

Peel the zest of the oranges and set aside. Peel away the remaining white membrane and discard. Chop oranges and set aside. Rinse and sort cranberries and set aside.

In a food processor with a sharp blade, combine orange zest and sugar. Pulse until zest is finely ground. Add cranberries and chop coarsely. Pour mixture into a bowl, add oranges, and toss. Store in the refrigerator for up to 4 weeks.

Makes about 3 cups

Raspberry Barbecue Sauce

Fruity barbecue sauces are wonderful glazes on grilled sausage, poultry, game, and pork.

1 package (10 ounces) frozen raspberries

2 cups barbecue sauce

2 tablespoons brown sugar

Thaw the raspberries and combine all of the ingredients in a glass jar. Store in the refrigerator for up to 3 weeks.

Makes about 3 cups

Raspberry-Jalapeño Sauce

Make your own raspberry barbecue sauce by adding 1/4 cup heated raspberry preserves to one cup of your favorite spicy tomato-based barbecue sauce.

1 bottle raspberry barbecue sauce

1 jalapeño, finely minced, or to taste

Combine the ingredients in a glass bowl and serve as a dipping sauce.

Makes 1 bottle of sauce

APRICOT GLAZE FOR HAM

This is a lovely sweet glaze that works well with pork and poultry. Serve the ham with grilled fresh asparagus topped with shaved Parmesan cheese and crusty artisan bread.

2 cups apricot preserves

1½ tablespoons cider vinegar

1 tablespoon ground cloves

2½ teaspoons dry mustard

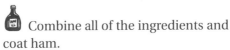 Combine all of the ingredients and coat ham.

Makes about 2 cups

TANGY APRICOT SAUCE

This is delicious with all types of poultry and pork.

1 jar (12 ounces) apricot preserves
2 tablespoons rice vinegar
1 tablespoon soy sauce

 Combine all of the ingredients.

Makes about 1¹/₂ cups

Que Queen Royal Jelly

*This peachy barbecue sauce is adapted
from Que Queen Lou Jane Temple's recipe
in her culinary mystery* Revenge of the
Barbeque Queens.

1 can (7 3/4 ounces) cling peaches
    with the syrup

6 cloves roasted garlic

1/2 cup orange juice

1/2 cup apple cider vinegar

1/2 cup ketchup

1/2 cup Dijon mustard

1/4 cup honey

1/4 cup peach preserves

1 tablespoon hot sauce

1 tablespoon dry mustard

1 teaspoon white pepper

1 teaspoon kosher salt

 In a food processor, purée the peaches and roasted garlic. Pour purée along with the remaining ingredients into a large saucepan. Simmer for 25 minutes, stirring often with a wooden spoon. The mixture will thicken and be a golden, light orange. Store in a jar in the refrigerator.

Makes about 3½ cups

QUICK PLUM SAUCE

This recipe adapts easily. Substitute apricot, peach, red currant, red raspberry, or black raspberry for the plum preserves or jam.

1/2 cup plum preserves or jam

1 tablespoon white vinegar

1 tablespoon soy sauce

1 clove garlic, minced

1/8 teaspoon ground ginger

Pinch of red pepper flakes

 In a small saucepan, combine all of the ingredients. Bring mixture to a boil over medium heat, stirring constantly. Remove from heat and cool before serving. Store in an airtight jar in the refrigerator for up to several weeks.

Makes about 2/3 cup

APRICOT-PLUM SAUCE

Serve with chicken, turkey, quail, or other game birds.

1 cup plum jelly or jam

1/2 cup apricot preserves

1 teaspoon white vinegar

1 teaspoon sugar

Combine all of the ingredients in a blender or food processor. Cover and refrigerate until ready to use. Store in an airtight jar in the refrigerator for up to several weeks.

Makes 1 1/2 cups

DIPPING SAUCE FOR GRILLED VEGETABLES

This is a wonderful quick sauce for grilled or steamed vegetables like asparagus, artichokes, broccoli, cauliflower, and green beans. It's also great with shellfish.

1 cup mayonnaise (do not substitute low-fat or fat-free)

1/3 cup Dijon mustard or other dark mustard

1 tablespoon lemon juice or more to thin

 In a small bowl, combine all of the ingredients. Store in an airtight container in the refrigerator for up to 3 weeks.

Makes about 1 1/3 cups

BOOKS ON BARBECUE

The popularity of cookbooks available for grill and barbecue enthusiasts is ever growing. Here is a list of favorites, some old and some new. For a complete list of titles on outdoor cooking, visit www.pigoutpublications.com.

Barbecue America by Rick Browne & Jack Bettridge
(1999, Time Life Books)
Barbecue Bible by Steven Raichlen (1998, Workman Publishing)
Barbecue Inferno by Dave DeWitt (2000, Ten Speed Press)
Barbecuing & Sausage Making Secrets by Charlie and Ruthie Knote
(1993, Culinary Institute of Smoke Cooking)
Great BBQ Sauce Book by Ardie Davis (1999, Ten Speed Press)
Great Ribs Book by Hugh Carpenter and Teri Sandison
(1999, Ten Speed Press)
Hooked on Fish on the Grill by Karen Adler (1992, Pig Out Publications)
Hot Barbecue! by Hugh Carpenter and Teri Sandison
(1996, Ten Speed Press)
Grilling Encyclopedia by A. Cort Sinnes (1992, Atlantic Monthly Press)
Indian Grill by Smita Chandra (1999, Harper Collins)
Passion of Barbeque by the Kansas City Barbeque Society
(1992, Hyperion)
Que Queens–Easy Grilling & Simple Smoking by Karen Adler &
Judith Fertig (1997, Pig Out Publications)
Smoke & Spice by Cheryl and Bill Jamison
(1995, Harvard Common Press)
Wild about Kansas City Barbecue by Rich Davis and Shifra Stein
(2000, Pig Out Publications)

CONVERSIONS

LIQUID
1 tablespoon = 15 milliliters
$^1/_2$ cup = 4 fluid ounces = 125 milliliters
1 cup = 8 fluid ounces = 250 milliliters

DRY
$^1/_4$ cup = 4 tablespoons = 2 ounces = 60 grams
1 cup = $^1/_2$ pound = 8 ounces = 250 grams

FLOUR
$^1/_2$ cup = 60 grams
1 cup = 4 ounces = 125 grams

TEMPERATURE
400 degrees F = 200 degrees C = gas mark 6
375 degrees F = 190 degrees C = gas mark 5
350 degrees F = 175 degrees C = gas mark 4

MISCELLANEOUS
2 tablespoons butter = 1 ounce = 30 grams
1 inch = 2.5 centimeters
all purpose flour = plain flour
baking soda = bicarbonate of soda
brown sugar= demerara sugar
confectioners' sugar = icing sugar
heavy cream = double cream
molasses= black treacle
raisins = sultanas
rolled oats = oat flakes
semisweet chocolate = plain chocol
sugar= caster sugar